I0426042

September 2012

WARFIGHTER SUPPORT

DOD Should Improve Development of Camouflage Uniforms and Enhance Collaboration Among the Services

G A O

Accountability ★ Integrity ★ Reliability

GAO-12-707

WARFIGHTER SUPPORT

DOD Should Improve Development of Camouflage Uniforms and Enhance Collaboration Among the Services

Highlights of GAO-12-707, a report to congressional requesters

Why GAO Did This Study

Since 2002, the military services have introduced seven new camouflage uniforms with varying patterns and colors—two desert, two woodland, and three universal. In addition, the Army is developing new uniform options and estimates it may cost up to $4 billion over 5 years to replace its current uniform and associated protective gear. GAO was asked to review the services' development of new camouflage uniforms. This report addresses: 1) the extent to which DOD guidance provides a consistent decision process to ensure new camouflage uniforms meet operational requirements and 2) the extent to which the services have used a joint approach to develop criteria, ensure equivalent protection and manage costs. To do this, GAO reviewed DOD, Office of Management and Budget (OMB) and GAO acquisition guidance and key practices, statutory requirements and policies, interviewed defense officials, and collected and analyzed records about uniform development.

What GAO Recommends

GAO recommends that DOD take four actions to improve the development of camouflage uniforms and enhance collaboration among the services: ensure that the services have and use clear policies and procedures and a knowledge-based approach, establish joint criteria, develop policy to ensure equivalent protection levels, and pursue partnerships where applicable to help reduce costs. DOD concurred with GAO's recommendations and identified planned actions.

View GAO-12-707.
For more information, contact Cary Russell at (202) 512-5431 or russellc@gao.gov.

What GAO Found

The military services have a degree of discretion regarding whether and how to apply Department of Defense (DOD) acquisition guidance for their uniform development and they varied in their usage of that guidance. As a result, the services had fragmented procedures for managing their uniform development programs, and did not consistently develop effective camouflage uniforms. GAO identified two key elements that are essential for producing successful outcomes in acquisitions: 1) using clear policies and procedures that are implemented consistently, and 2) obtaining effective information to make decisions, such as credible, reliable, and timely data. The Marine Corps followed these two key elements to produce a successful outcome, and developed a uniform that met its requirements. By contrast, two other services, the Army and Air Force, did not follow the two key elements; both services developed uniforms that did not meet mission requirements and had to replace them. Without additional guidance from DOD on the use of clear policies and procedures and a knowledge-based approach, the services may lack assurance that they have a disciplined approach to set requirements and develop new uniforms that meet operational needs.

The military services' fragmented approach for acquiring uniforms has not ensured the development of joint criteria for new uniforms or achieved cost efficiency. DOD has not met a statutory requirement to establish joint criteria for future uniforms or taken steps to ensure that uniforms provide equivalent levels of performance and protection for service members, and the services have not pursued opportunities to seek to reduce clothing costs, such as by collaborating on uniform inventory costs. The National Defense Authorization Act for Fiscal Year 2010 required the military departments to establish joint criteria for future ground combat uniforms. The departments asked the Joint Clothing and Textiles Governance Board to develop the joint criteria, but the task is incomplete. If the services do not use joint criteria to guide their activities, one or more service may develop uniforms without certainty that the uniforms include the newest technology, advanced materials or designs, and meet an acceptable level of performance. Further, DOD does not have a means to ensure that the services meet statutory policy permitting the development of service-unique uniforms as long as the uniforms, to the maximum extent practicable, provide service members the equivalent levels of performance and protection and minimize the risk to individuals operating in the joint battle space. Without a policy to ensure that services develop and field uniforms with equivalent performance and protection, the services could fall short of protecting all service members equally, potentially exposing a number to unnecessary risks. Finally, the services may have opportunities for partnerships to reduce inventory costs for new uniforms. The Army may be able to save about $82 million if it can partner with another service. Under DOD guidance, the services are encouraged to actively seek to reduce costs. The Air Force has shown interest in the Army's current uniform development, but none of the services has agreed to partner with the Army on a new uniform. In the absence of a DOD requirement that the services collaborate to standardize the development and introduction of camouflage uniforms, the services may forego millions of dollars in potential cost savings.

Contents

Abbreviations

ABU	Airman Battle Uniform
ABE	Airman Battle Ensemble
ABS-G	Airman Battle System-Ground
ACU	Army Combat Uniform
AT&L	Acquisition, Technology, and Logistics
BDU	Battle Dress Uniform
DCU	Desert Combat Uniform
DLA	Defense Logistics Agency
DOD	Department of Defense
FR ACU	Flame Resistant Army Combat Uniform
FROG	Flame Resistant Organizational Gear
IED	Improvised Explosive Device
MARPAT	Marine Corps Pattern
MCCUU	Marine Corps Combat Utility Uniform
MDA	Milestone Decision Authority
MP-ICE	Program Manager-Infantry Combat Equipment
OCP	Operation Enduring Freedom Camouflage Pattern
OMB	Office of Management and Budget
PEO	Program Executive Office

United States Government Accountability Office
Washington, DC 20548

September 28, 2012

The Honorable Claire McCaskill
Chairman
The Honorable Kelly Ayotte
Ranking Member
Subcommittee on Readiness
  and Management Support
Committee on Armed Services
United States Senate

The Honorable Richard Burr
United States Senate

The military services spent about $300 million in Fiscal Year 2011 to procure new camouflage uniforms. The primary goal of camouflage is to reduce vulnerability of forces to detection in combat; however, over time the services also have chosen camouflage patterns that are service specific and distinguish one service from another. Since 2002, the services have introduced seven new camouflage uniforms with varying patterns and colors—two desert, two woodland, and three universal.[1] In addition, each service has introduced a service-specific flame-resistant uniform in response to urgent warfighter needs. Most of the services' new camouflage patterns and colors replaced two Army-developed camouflage patterns that all military services were using.[2] Specifically, the services replaced the Army's four-color woodland camouflage pattern developed in 1981, known as the Battle Dress Uniform or Combat Utility Uniform, and its three-color desert camouflage pattern developed in early 1990 and known as the Desert Camouflage Uniform. Further, as part of the Army's ongoing camouflage study, the office responsible for uniforms, Program Executive Office (PEO) Soldier, plans to present the results of its camouflage testing to senior leadership by the end of December 2012 on future uniform options. If the Army selects a new uniform, officials

---

[1]A universal camouflage pattern is designed to blend across terrains such as woodland, urban, and desert.

[2]One camouflage pattern, the Operation Enduring Freedom Camouflage Pattern, replaced the Army Combat Uniform in Afghanistan.

estimated that it may cost up to $4 billion over 5 years to replace a new camouflage uniform and associated protective gear for the entire service.

In May 2010, we reported on the Department of Defense's (DOD) use of ground combat uniforms in response to a mandate in the National Defense Authorization Act for Fiscal Year 2010.[3] We reported that combat uniform performance standards developed by some of the services were not related to specific combat environments; the introduction of flame-resistant fabric, insect repellent treatment, and the increased pace of operations in Afghanistan accounted for increases in uniform production and procurement costs; and government-owned patents on elements of the Marine Corps' uniforms presented no legal barrier to allowing other services to use these elements. In June 2011, we reported on matters related to the supply of flame resistant fibers for the production of military uniforms.[4] In response to your request, this report addresses 1) the extent to which DOD guidance provides a consistent decision process to ensure new camouflage uniforms meet operational requirements and 2) the extent to which the services have used a joint approach to develop criteria, ensure equivalent protection, and manage costs.

To determine the extent to which DOD guidance ensures the services follow a consistent decision process to guide the development and acquisition of their camouflage uniforms, we reviewed key guidance and service decision-making processes. We reviewed key practices for federal acquisitions that are included in the Office of Management and Budget's (OMB) guidelines and GAO's framework for assessing acquisition functions.[5] We compared OMB's and GAO's key elements for acquisitions with the decision processes used by the services, and we identified two elements that are essential for agencies to follow to

---

[3]GAO, *Warfighter Support: Observations on DOD's Ground Combat Uniforms,* GAO-10-669R (Washington, D.C.: May 28, 2010). The report followed a briefing provided to the committees in April 2010 to fulfill the mandate found in section 352 of the Act. *See* Pub. L. No. 111-84, § 352(b), (c) (2009) (10 U.S.C. § 771 note prec.).

[4]GAO, *Military Uniforms: Issues Related to the Supply of Flame Resistant Fibers for the Production of Military Uniforms,* GAO-11-682R (Washington, D.C.: June 30, 2011).

[5]Executive Office of the President, Office of Management and Budget, Office of Federal Procurement Policy, Guidelines for Assessing the Acquisition Function (May 2008); GAO, *Framework for Assessing the Acquisition Function at Federal Agencies,* GAO-05-218G (Washington, D.C.: September 2005).

produce successful outcomes and were applicable to uniform-development programs. The two elements are clear policies and procedures that are implemented consistently and a knowledge-based approach that includes meaningful data to determine whether a product will meet customer requirements. Additionally, we interviewed relevant DOD and military service officials, including military service officials responsible for the management of uniform development and acquisition policy. Further, we interviewed officials from the Office of the Under Secretary of Defense for Acquisition, Technology, and Logistics about the relevance and flexibility of DOD's acquisition guidance and how the services used this or other guidance in their development decisions. We visited the Army, Marine Corps, Air Force, and Navy offices responsible for managing the development or acquisition of its camouflage uniforms and gathered and analyzed data on the use of policies to support their decision processes and the testing or cost data that guided decisions during the development of their camouflage uniforms.

To determine the extent to which the services have used a joint approach to develop criteria, ensure equivalent protection and manage costs, we reviewed requirements and policies found in DOD guidance and in the National Defense Authorization Act for Fiscal Year 2010.[6] We also reviewed data and interviewed officials from the military services and members of the Joint Clothing and Textiles Governance Board to determine if the services had established criteria for camouflage uniforms using a joint approach. In addition, we assessed information from DOD about how DOD officials plan to meet the statutory policy permitting future uniforms to uniquely reflect the identity of the individual services, as long as they provide equivalent levels of performance and protection to the maximum extent practicable. Finally, we reviewed guidance and interviewed officials with the Defense Logistics Agency, Troop Support office to assess how they encourage the services to jointly reduce development and acquisition costs. Our detailed scope and methodology appears in Appendix I.

We conducted this performance audit from September 2010 to September 2012 in accordance with generally accepted government auditing standards. These standards require that we plan and perform the audit to obtain sufficient, appropriate evidence to provide a reasonable

---

[6]*See* Pub. L. No. 111-84, § 352(a), (d).

basis for our findings and conclusions based on our audit objectives. We believe that the evidence obtained provides a reasonable basis for our findings and conclusions based on our audit objectives.

Background

Military Services' Camouflage Uniforms

Each service has introduced at least one new uniform into inventory in the last 10 years. Prior to 2002, all four military services were using the Army's Battle Dress and Desert Camouflage uniforms. However, since that time each of the services (including the Army) has developed new uniforms to address deficiencies that they identified with the existing Army uniforms. Improvements incorporated into the design of the services' new uniforms include improved visual or near-infrared capabilities for concealment and improved fabric technology. Additionally, each service introduced a service-specific flame resistant uniform in response to urgent need requests. For additional information on the development of flame resistant uniforms by the services, see appendix II. The services also expected the new uniforms to provide other benefits, such as a unique appearance to increase the morale of personnel and aid in recruitment. Figure 1 provides additional information on the development of the services' uniforms and is followed by a description of each service's development activities.

Figure 1: Services' Camouflage Uniforms, Dates of Initiation and Fielding, and Development Costs

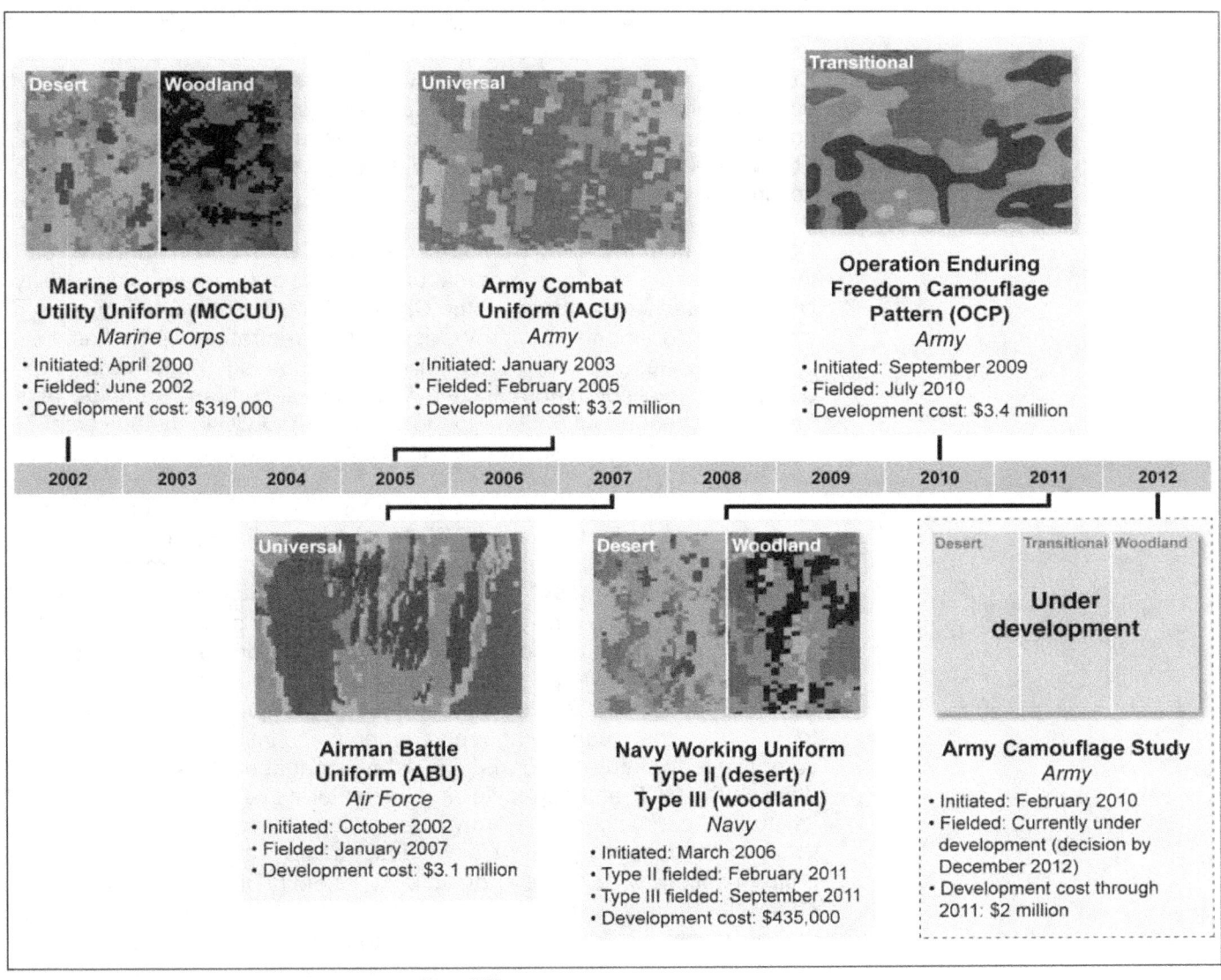

Source: DOD.

Marine Corps	In April 2000, the Commandant of the Marine Corps directed the development and fielding of a new Marine Corps Combat Utility Uniform (MCCUU). The requirements of the new uniform, developed under the decision-making authority of the Commander of the Marine Corps System Command, were to provide Marines with a uniform that increased durability and combat utility compared to the current uniform, provide commanders versatility for a variety of missions, and be uniquely Marine. The Marine Corps spent $319,000 to develop the MCCUU, and began fielding its new uniforms in June 2002.

Army

Development of the Army Combat Uniform (ACU) began in January 2003 in response to a need for a combat uniform with greater operational utility. Under the decision authority of the Chief of Staff, the new uniform included requirements to improve visual or near-infrared capabilities, to improve morale, and to provide a universal camouflage pattern with acceptable levels of performance in woodland, desert, and urban terrains. The Army spent about $3.2 million to develop the ACU in the universal camouflage pattern and began fielding its new uniform in February 2005.

In 2009, based on concerns from soldiers in Afghanistan, a congressional conference committee directed DOD to take immediate action to provide personnel deployed to Afghanistan with a camouflage pattern that was suited to that environment.[7] The conference committee further directed the Secretary of the Army to provide a report on the program plans and budgetary adjustments necessary to provide appropriate uniforms to deployed and deploying troops to Afghanistan. In response, the Army developed the Operation Enduring Freedom Camouflage Pattern (OCP) to address current camouflage requirements and initiated a study of camouflage for future uniforms. The Army spent about $3.4 million to develop the OCP and began fielding the uniform in July 2010. As part of its study of camouflage, the Army is reviewing camouflage to identify three color variations—desert, woodland, and transitional[8]—as future uniform options. Additionally, the study will identify one camouflage pattern for protective gear that blends well with all three uniforms. By the end of December 2012, the Army plans to brief senior Army leadership on

---

[7]See H.R. Rep. No. 111-151, at 86 (2009) (Conf. Rep., accompanying the Supplemental Appropriations Act, 2009).

[8]A transitional camouflage pattern, similar to the universal camouflage pattern, is designed for multiple geographic environments.

the results of its study. The Army spent about $2 million through Fiscal Year 2011 on the development of these uniforms, and reported in February 2012 that it expects to spend an additional $5 million on development costs through Fiscal Year 2017. If the Army chooses a new camouflage uniform, officials estimate that it may cost up to $4 billion over 5 years to replace its uniform and related protective gear.

Air Force

The Chief of Staff of the Air Force in October 2002 initiated a research and development project to field a new uniform. The objective was to design a distinctive uniform that—compared to the current Army Battle Dress Uniform (BDU)—provided a better fit, and was also easier and less costly to maintain.[9] According to officials, the program was conducted under the authority of the Chief of Staff. The Air Force spent about $3.2 million on the development of the Airman Battle Uniform (ABU) and began fielding its new uniform in January 2007.

Navy

In 2006, as part of a broader review of Navy uniforms, the Chief of Naval Operations announced approval of a concept for new desert and woodland[10] uniforms for Navy ground forces.[11] In 2009, the Chief of Naval Operations received approval from Special Operations Command to use camouflage patterns, developed by Naval Special Warfare Command,[12] for the Navy's new Type II desert and Type III woodland uniforms. The Commander, Naval Facilities Engineering Command, oversaw the $435,000 spent by the Navy on the final design of its two new camouflage uniforms. The Navy began fielding its Type II desert uniform in February 2011 and its Type III woodland uniform in September 2011.

---

[9]The BDU was not permanent pressed and needed either to be ironed after laundering or to be professionally dry cleaned to maintain an acceptable appearance during duty at bases, according to Air Force officials.

[10]The desert uniform is designed for desert, tundra, and arid regions; the woodland uniform is designed for jungle, woodland, and temperate regions.

[11]The Navy also developed its Navy Working Uniform Type I in a blue, digital pattern, but designated it for sailors at sea and ashore. It is not considered a ground combat or utility uniform, and consequently we did not include it as part of this review.

[12]Independent of the Navy costs, Naval Special Warfare spent around $8 million overall on the development of its Personal Signature Management program, of which its camouflage uniforms were one component.

GAO-12-707 Warfighter Support

DOD Policies

DOD's acquisition guidance, collectively referred to as the 5000 series,[13] provides management principles, policies, and procedures to establish and manage acquisition programs and to help to manage the nation's investments in technologies, programs, and products. The primary objective of defense acquisition is to acquire quality products that satisfy user needs with measurable improvements to mission capability and operational support, and to do so in a timely manner and at a fair and reasonable price. The military departments have issued guidance to implement the DOD guidance.[14] According to DOD Directive 5000.01, *The Defense Acquisition System,* an acquisition program is a directed, funded effort that provides a new, improved or continuing materiel, weapon or information system, or service capability in response to an approved need. DOD Instruction 5000.02, *Operation of the Defense Acquisition System*, establishes a flexible management framework for translating capability needs and technology opportunities into acquisition programs.

In addition, the instruction identifies specific statutory and regulatory reports and information—such as an acquisition strategy, cost estimates, test and evaluation activities, and risk assessments throughout the process to support decisions from design to production.[15] A key tenet of the guidance is that it provides the approving official, the Milestone Decision Authority (MDA), with the discretion to structure the activities and reporting requirements of the acquisition process as appropriate and

---

[13]The 5000 series includes Department of Defense Directive 5000.01, *The Defense Acquisition System* (May 12, 2003) (certified current as of Nov. 20, 2007); Department of Defense Instruction 5000.02, *Operation of the Defense Acquisition System* (Dec. 8, 2008); and the *Defense Acquisition Guidebook*, which supports the guidance by providing background information, tutorial discussions, key practices, and information about requirements for each phase and milestone decision.

[14]The military departments' implementing guidance includes Army Regulation 70-1, Army Acquisition Policy (July 22, 2011); Secretary of the Navy Instruction 5000.2E, *Implementation and Operation of the Defense Acquisition System and the Joint Capabilities Integration and Development System* (Sept. 1, 2011); and Air Force Instruction 63-101, *Acquisition and Sustainment Life Cycle Management* (Apr. 8, 2009) (incorporating through change 4, Aug. 3, 2011).

[15]DOD has issued guidance that amplifies and amends the requirements found in DOD Instruction 5000.02. *See, e.g.,* Directive Type Memorandum 11-003, *Reliability Analysis, Planning, Tracking, and Reporting* (Mar. 21, 2011); Directive Type Memorandum 09-027, *Implementation of the Weapon Systems Acquisition Reform Act of 2009* (Dec. 4, 2009).

consistent with statutory and regulatory requirements to achieve performance, schedule, and cost goals.

Under another DOD Regulation, DOD 4140.1-R, DOD provides guidance on the development to the delivery of items, and on the key practices in materiel management within DOD's supply chain framework.[16] For uniforms and other clothing and textiles, the regulation includes procedures on coordination of research and testing activities. It also encourages DOD components to actively seek to reduce costs by standardizing basic materials and accessories, such as new clothing items,[17] and provides information on costs to introduce a new uniform into inventory. According to Defense Logistics Agency policy, an initial inventory fee could apply to new items when the cost of introducing a replacement item into inventory is greater than 10 percent of the cost of the item being replaced or when a new item is introduced by an individual organization.[18] The initial inventory fee, charged by the Defense Logistics Agency, covers the cost of acquiring initial inventory of seven months of the new clothing and the cost of the remaining inventory being replaced.

Also, DOD issued Instruction 4140.63, *Management of DOD Clothing and Textiles (Class II)*, in August 2008, in part to prescribe authority, policy, and responsibilities for the management of clothing and textiles in peacetime and across the spectrum of military operations.[19] The instruction directed the establishment of the Joint Clothing and Textiles Governance Board and also made the Director of the Defense Logistics

---

[16]*See generally* Department of Defense Regulation 4140.1-R, *DOD Supply Chain Materiel Management Regulation* (May 23, 2003).

[17]With respect to clothing items, including combat and individual equipment, the regulation encourages standardization insofar as functionality, maintenance of combat readiness, and mission accomplishment permit. The regulation states that any desired distinctiveness should be obtained by using separate items of insignia, patches, etc. *See id.*, para. C8.2.2.4.1.

[18]For new clothing with a forecasted total annual demand value exceeding $100,000, DOD policy provides that the initial investment and acquisition of inventory levels to satisfy demands up to the effective date of supply is the financial responsibility of the requesting component. Officials of the Defense Logistics Agency, Troop Support office stated that their interpretation of the policy is that items with a value of 10 percent greater than the item being replaced will include the initial inventory fee.

[19]*See* Department of Defense Instruction 4140.63, *Management of DOD Clothing and Textiles (Class II)* (Aug. 5, 2008).

Agency responsible for ensuring collaboration and DOD-wide integration of clothing and textiles activities by establishing and chairing the board. The governance board includes representation from the Office of the Deputy Assistant Secretary of Defense for Supply Chain Integration and logistics officials from the Joint Chiefs of Staff, military services, and the Defense Logistics Agency.

DOD Instruction 4140.63 also describes responsibilities of various DOD entities in the development, management, and use of clothing and textiles. Clothing and textiles covered by the instruction include uniforms, other personal items, and organizational clothing and individual equipment that belong to the organization and not to the person using it. In addition, the instruction prescribes policy that the military departments maintain responsibility for the acquisition, funding, and fielding of new clothing and textiles in accordance with the management principles, policies, and procedures in DOD Directive 5000.01, *The Defense Acquisition System*. Finally, Instruction 4140.63 directs the military departments to coordinate operational requirements and sourcing with the Director of the Defense Logistics Agency to minimize duplication and redundancy.

National Defense Authorization Act for Fiscal Year 2010

The National Defense Authorization Act for Fiscal Year 2010 requires the Secretaries of the military departments to establish joint criteria for future ground combat uniforms.[20] According to the act, the joint criteria shall ensure that new technologies, advanced materials, and other advances in ground combat uniform design may be shared between the military services and are not precluded from being adapted for use by any military service due to service-specific proprietary arrangements. The act also established United States policy that the design and fielding of future ground combat uniforms may uniquely reflect the identities of the individual military services as long as the uniforms, to the maximum extent practicable, provide equivalent levels of performance and protection for members commensurate with their respective assigned

---

[20]*See* Pub. L. No. 111-84, § 352(d).

combat missions and minimize the risk to the individual soldier, sailor, airman, or marine operating in the joint battle space.[21]

Military Services Have Not Used a Consistent Decision-Making Process to Produce Effective Camouflage Uniforms

The military services have a degree of discretion regarding whether and how to apply acquisition guidance for their uniform development, and varied in their use of the guidance. DOD provided no alternative or additional direction clarifying use of acquisition guidance or other guidance when developing ground combat uniforms. Consequently, the services used varying, fragmented processes for managing their uniform acquisition activities, which have not consistently ensured the development of effective camouflage uniforms.

DOD, OMB and GAO Have Provided Guidance and Key Practices for Effective Acquisition Processes

DOD has provided policy, known as the 5000 series, which is designed to offer the services a flexible management framework for translating capability needs and technology opportunities into stable, affordable, and well-managed acquisition programs. In the context of their uniform development activities, the services varied in their views as to the applicability of the 5000 series. For example, the Air Force did not view its uniform development and fielding activities as an acquisition program, although it may do so in the future as a consequence of the policy contained in DOD Instruction 4140.63.[22] The services also varied in their usage of the acquisition guidance where they determined that it applied. Under the guidance, the milestone decision authority may tailor the regulatory information requirements and acquisition process to achieve cost, schedule, and performance goals, where consistent with statutory and regulatory requirements. Generally, due to statutory and regulatory

---

[21]See § 352(a). Under the policy, service-unique uniforms would, to the maximum extent practicable: (1) provide members of every military service an equivalent level of performance, functionality, and protection commensurate with their respective assigned combat missions; (2) minimize risk to the individual soldier, sailor, airman, or marine operating in the joint battle space; and (3) provide interoperability with other components of individual war fighter systems, including body armor and other individual protective systems. See id.

[22]The instruction prescribes policy that the military departments maintain responsibility for the acquisition, funding, and fielding of new clothing and textiles in accordance with the management principles, policies, and procedures in DOD Directive 5000.01. See Department of Defense Instruction 4140.63, Management of DOD Clothing and Textiles (Class II), para. 4(b) (Aug. 5, 2008).

requirements, higher-cost acquisition programs have greater information, reporting, and procedural requirements than lower-cost programs. Accordingly, since milestone decision authorities that manage lower-cost programs generally have fewer statutory or regulatory requirements to implement, they often have greater flexibility to tailor the guidance. Due to the flexibility allowed in DOD's acquisition guidance and varied views as to its applicability to uniform development programs, we also evaluated key practices in the Office of Management and Budget's guidance to federal acquisition officers on steps to take to assess and achieve efficient and effective acquisition functions. OMB's guidance noted that it was adopting key practices that we reported in 2005, which listed a framework of cornerstones and elements for an effective acquisition function.[23]

Specifically, for this review we identified two elements from the OMB and GAO guidance that we considered essential for agencies to follow to produce successful outcomes because the two elements most closely relate to product development activities. The two elements are: clear policies and procedures that are implemented consistently, and a knowledge-based approach that includes meaningful data to determine whether a product will meet customer requirements. We assessed whether three services—the Marine Corps, Army and Air Force—followed two key elements that OMB and GAO have determined are key practices for a decision-making process that produces successful outcomes, and to what extent each service developed uniforms that met requirements. We did not assess the Navy's decision process because it adopted uniforms developed by Naval Special Warfare Command rather than developing a new uniform. The development activities of special operation forces, such as the Naval Special Warfare Command, are outside the scope of this review. We were not requested to review the uniform program for special forces.

---

[23]Executive Office of the President, Office of Management and Budget, Office of Federal Procurement Policy, *Guidelines for Assessing the Acquisition Function* (May 2008); GAO-05-218G.

Services Varied in their Decision-Making Processes for Acquisitions, and Two New Uniforms Did Not Meet Specific Mission Requirements

The services' decision-making processes for developing new uniforms are fragmented and vary in their effectiveness. The Marine Corps used a decision process that followed the two key elements that we identified as essential to produce a successful acquisition outcome, and produced a combat uniform that the Marine Corps officials have found effective. However, the Army and Air Force did not follow the two key elements, and they found that their new uniforms did not meet specific mission requirements. To meet combat requirements, both the Army and Air Force replaced their uniforms for personnel deployed to Afghanistan with the OCP uniform.

Without additional guidance from DOD on the use of clear policies and procedures for a knowledge-based approach to developing effective uniforms, some services may continue to lack assurance that they have a disciplined process that is capable of delivering uniforms that meet warfighter requirements.

Marine Corps' Decision Process Used Elements Essential For a Successful Outcome

Marine Corps officials used a decision process that followed two key elements we found essential to produce a successful acquisition outcome, and produced a combat uniform that the Marine Corps officials have found effective and continues to meet Marines' needs. The Marine Corps officials used clear policies and procedures that were implemented consistently, and used a knowledge-based approach that included collection and use of meaningful data to determine whether a product will meet warfighter requirements.

Regarding clear policies and procedures, according to officials, the Marine Corps used the flexible decision framework provided by then-current versions of DOD's and the Secretary of the Navy's acquisition guidance to establish a process designed to ensure that its decisions would result in a camouflage uniform that met its requirements.[24] In doing so, the Marine Corps developed a number of key documents as tools to support acquisition planning and decision making. For example, the Marine Corps developed documents to support decision making in the five areas described below.

---

[24]According to officials, the Marine Corps used Department of Defense Instruction 5000.2, *Operation of the Defense Acquisition System* (Jan. 4, 2001) and Secretary of the Navy Instruction 5000.2B, *Implementation of Mandatory Procedures for Major and Non-Major Defense Acquisition Programs and Major and Non-Major Information Technology Acquisition Programs* (Dec. 6, 1996). These publications have since been superseded.

- *Acquisition Strategy*—First, officials used an acquisition strategy to highlight deficiencies in the service's current uniform and assessed methods for addressing the deficiencies. The service considered modifying the current uniform or buying a commercially available uniform, but concluded that the best approach was to begin a new development program that could rapidly test and evaluate prototypes of alternative designs that would meet Marine preferences obtained from field surveys and allow it to develop a unique uniform for the Marine Corps. Officials provided an action plan and key dates for developmental testing, testing of prototypes, field evaluations, production approval, contract award, first article testing, product verification, full production, initial issuance, and initial operational capability. Also, the strategy included contracting requirements and a phased fielding plan to test small lots of uniforms for a limited number of Marines before building up inventory to meet the needs of all Marines.

- *Acquisition Program Baseline*—The Marine Corps developed an acquisition program baseline to seek and receive full funding for new uniforms, and to list performance, schedule, and cost parameters over the program's life cycle.

- *Risk Assessment*—In preparing a risk assessment, the Marine Corps concluded that risk to cost, schedule, and performance would be low. The assessment included a 20-year life cycle cost estimate for the uniform. Further, the scheduled fielding of the uniform would be deliberately slow to build up inventory before changing over to the new uniform. The new uniforms were developed with Marine input both at the conceptual and developmental phases, and the uniforms were updated based on field input during the first phase of fielding.

- *Cost Estimate for Program's Life Cycle*—The Marine Corps chose to prepare a life-cycle cost estimate for the program. Life-cycle costs include research and development, investment, operation and support, and disposal. The life-cycle cost analysis was used to assess program affordability and to support the review and oversight of cost estimates. Among various assumptions of costs, Marine Corps officials determined that the 2001 projections of the number of officer candidates and active and reserve recruits would remain constant throughout the 20-year life cycle. All told, the Marine Corps estimated that the 20-year life-cycle costs would be about $502 million in constant fiscal year 2001 dollars.

- *Test and Evaluation Master Plan*—The Marine Corps Systems Command created a plan to evaluate different camouflage patterns and colors. Marine Corps Systems Command and U.S. Army Soldier, Biological and Chemical Command, conducted testing and evaluation on camouflage technology and alternative uniform designs to determine which camouflage and elements of uniform design would meet user requirements. The plan also included field tests by approximately 450 Marines to evaluate two designs of the new uniform for suitability for a number of mission-oriented tasks, such as helicopter and amphibious operations. The planned tests and evaluations were to determine durability, function, and preferred features.

In addition, Marine Corps officials established a process that followed the federal key practice to use a knowledge-based approach that includes meaningful data to determine whether a product will meet customer requirements. A knowledge-based approach includes obtaining sufficient information about technology, design options, and production capabilities so that the product will be able to meet various requirements. In April 2000, according to documents, Marine Corps officials decided to replace the existing combat uniforms with new camouflage combat uniforms to increase durability and utility for combat over the current BDU and Desert Camouflage Uniform and to provide Marines with a unique and distinct combat uniform.

As part of their knowledge-based approach during decision making, Marine Corps officials considered about 70 camouflage patterns, and Marine Corps test observers, who were assessing the effectiveness of the camouflage, narrowed the candidates to eight. The eight were narrowed to the top three performers, due to what Marine Corps officials described as patent issues. The Marine Corps chose four colors each for the patterns for woodland and desert environments based on discussions with camouflage experts. The Marine Corps Commandant reviewed the camouflage patterns and officials chose two camouflage patterns for further testing—Tiger Stripe and Canadian Disruptive Pattern (later named the Marine Corps Pattern or MARPAT). However, initial field testing showed that the Tiger Stripe was not an effective camouflage pattern. After other field tests with woodland and desert colored variations of the Marine Corps Pattern, Marine Corps officials determined that the Marine Corps Pattern had performance advantages over the Tiger-Stripe pattern when used in camouflage uniforms. On the 7-point scale, with 7 being the most effective camouflage, test observers gave average scores of 5.0 to the Marine Corps Pattern and 4.16 to the Tiger Stripe. In June

2001, the Commander of the Marine Corps Systems Command approved the MARPAT camouflage pattern for production and deployment of the new MCCUU uniform.

During the field tests of the MCCUU, evaluators involved 284 Marines from Marine Expeditionary Forces for an average of 22 days in 2001. Wearers spent about 8 days in the field, and 14 days on base. The evaluation led by U.S. Army Soldier, Biological & Chemical Command, included the following results:

- Fit and Comfort: 76 percent were satisfied with the fit of the blouse and 64 percent were satisfied with the fit of the trousers. Overall, wearers gave both clothing items 6.3 comfort ratings toward the maximum positive rating of 7.

- Durability: 13 percent reported durability problems with the blouse, such as Velcro and snaps that did not hold or rips and tears. 25 percent reported durability problems with the trousers, such as excessive wear and rips at the knees (mostly caused by field training).

- Appearance: 98 percent stated the uniform generally was easy to care for and maintain, and about two-thirds of respondents stated that the uniform, after laundering, had creases that were sharp enough for garrison wear.

- Mission Suitability: 97 percent stated the uniform was suitable for use in a tactical environment.

As a result of the field testing, the service adopted the Marine Corps Pattern and uniform design in the production of its new camouflage uniforms.

Army's Decision Process Did Not Use Elements Essential For a Successful Outcome

The Army used a decision process for the development of a new uniform that did not produce a successful outcome, and it had to replace that uniform in 2010. The Army did not consistently use clear policies and procedures or use a knowledge-based approach that includes meaningful data to determine whether the product would meet customer requirements. Our prior work has shown that the use of policies, procedures, and a knowledge-based approach is essential to produce successful outcomes.[25] While the Army conducted some testing on camouflage patterns, it did not complete the testing before selecting a pattern. As a result, the Army developed a uniform that proved to provide ineffective concealment for operations in Afghanistan.

According to officials and documentation, during the decision process to develop the Army Combat Uniform (ACU)—which ran from 2003 to 2005—the Army used some elements of DOD's 5000-series policy and Army Regulation 70-1, which is the military department's implementing guidance. The Army identified the approval structure and decision maker for its development activities. However, the Army did not follow the 5000-series policy or establish alternate policies and procedures on reporting of testing, performance, and risk to the program to support its decision making, which could have provided reasonable assurance that its requirements were met. The Army tailored its development program in a manner that excluded steps in the process that might have ensured the use of test and evaluation results to support decision making throughout the development of the ACU. For example, the Army did not take steps to establish an acquisition strategy, which can guide the development activities, or use another mechanism to inform senior leadership about testing, performance, and risks associated with the development of the uniform. An acquisition strategy can provide a master schedule for research, development, testing, production, fielding and other activities; one of the keys to a successful program is an acquisition strategy that is carefully developed and consistently followed.

As part of our review, officials from the program office that managed the program—Program Executive Office (PEO) Soldier—told us that officials briefed the Chief of Staff in March 2004 through the Army Uniform Board on issues related to the management of fielding the new uniform to soldiers. Specifically, the briefing included the number of uniforms per soldier, the cost of the new uniforms, and the timeline for fielding. The Army did not provide information on testing results or an evaluation of the performance and risks associated with the development of the uniform. Developing an acquisition strategy could have provided the Army with a structured approach to requirements, testing plans, cost estimate data, a risk assessment of the program, and recommendations to support decision making.

---

[25]GAO-05-218G.

Similarly, we found that the Army did not employ the key practice of using a knowledge-based approach to support development decisions that included obtaining sufficient information about camouflage performance from testing data. As part of the development of the ACU, the Army Natick Soldier Research, Development, and Engineering Center began a field evaluation in 2002 of the performance of 13 camouflage patterns and color combinations. However, PEO Soldier officials told us that prior to the completion of this study the leadership chose a camouflage pattern and colors for the new uniform without data from the camouflage study. PEO Soldier leadership could not provide a performance report to support the selection of the Universal Camouflage Pattern nor explain how the camouflage pattern was developed. The Universal Camouflage Pattern was not part of the Natick study and was not tested prior to the decision by PEO Soldier to use this pattern or prior to the June 2004 approval of the pattern by the Chief of Staff. The Army began fielding the uniform in February 2005. Later in 2005, the Army Natick Soldier Research, Development, and Engineering Center completed its camouflage evaluation and recommended a different pattern—Desert Brush—as the most effective universal camouflage pattern. In 2009, a follow-on Army study found that the Universal Camouflage Pattern of the ACU offered less effective concealment than the patterns chosen by the Marine Corps and some foreign military services, such as Syria and China. The test showed that soldiers wearing the Universal ACU were at greater operational risk of visibility to enemy forces than soldiers wearing the Marines' pattern.

Moreover, soldiers deployed to Afghanistan conveyed concerns about their uniform, which they indicated provided ineffective concealment in the Afghan environment. In response to those concerns, in 2009 a congressional conference committee directed immediate action to provide combat uniforms suited to that environment.[26] The Army established a decision process that included a strategy of development and fielding activities and leadership review of the testing to support a decision on a new uniform. The Army expedited testing of camouflage patterns suited for Afghanistan by sending a photo simulation team to Afghanistan to collect environmental data. Further, the Army surveyed soldiers on

---

[26]See H.R. Rep. No. 111-151, at 86 (2009) (Conf. Rep., accompanying the Supplemental Appropriations Act, 2009).

deployment to support its decision making. The Army also considered the conclusions of the 2005 and 2009 Natick studies.

In 2010, the Army began replacing the ACU for personnel deployed to Afghanistan with Operation Enduring Freedom Camouflage Pattern (OCP), and estimated that the replacement would add more than $38.8 million in development and initial fielding costs for fiscal year 2010 and 2011.

For future uniform needs, the Army is conducting a study to choose environment-specific camouflage patterns for use Army-wide by the end of December 2012. If the Army chooses a new camouflage uniform, officials estimate that it may cost up to $4 billion over 5 years to replace its uniform and related protective gear. The leadership of PEO Soldier told us that, unlike the decision process used to support development of the camouflage pattern for the ACU, the decision process for future camouflage uniforms will include a knowledge-based approach and greater use of DOD policies and procedures to ensure that decisions are informed, science-based, and data driven. For example, the Army established an acquisition strategy for conducting the development of new uniforms, hosted regular meetings to obtain input from other services and Army organizations, and PEO Soldier regularly provided Army leadership with information about its development activities.

Air Force's Decision Process Did Not Use Elements Essential for a Successful Outcome

In 2002, Air Force officials began developing the Airman Battle Uniform (ABU) for noncombat use to replace two combat uniforms. At the time, the U.S. military, including the Air Force, was conducting expeditionary operations worldwide, including Afghanistan. Officials later recognized that the ABU under development might not meet their needs, and in 2005 they began testing to determine the suitability of the ABU in a combat environment. We found that the decision process used by the Air Force in the development of the ABU did not follow the key element of using clear policies and procedures. Also, the Air Force did not employ a knowledge-based approach including an analysis of the potential requirements for both combat and base uniforms. As a result, the Air Force developed a non-combat uniform for wear at the home base. Personnel found that the uniform's fabric weight was uncomfortable due to heat buildup, and the Air Force had to replace the uniform with one constructed from a lighter fabric.

During our review, Air Force officials told us that they did not follow DOD's 5000-series policies. According to Air Force officials, in 2002 Air Force leadership determined that its development activities for its new uniform—intended for use only on bases—did not constitute an acquisition program under the 5000 series and Air Force Instruction 63-101, entitled *Operations of Capabilities Based Acquisition System*. Instead of following a specific policy, the Chief of Staff provided direction on the development of the uniform during three senior leadership briefings between 2002 and 2004, according to Air Force officials. In considering support for his decision making, the Chief of Staff did not require the Clothing Office to establish a strategy to guide the development activities, such as documenting deficiencies of the current combat uniforms and establishing capability requirements for the replacement uniforms. Also, the Chief of Staff did not use a mechanism to report how the new uniform would meet capability requirements, as well as the results of uniform testing, performance evaluation, and risk assessment. All these procedures could have provided more reasonable assurance that personnel requirements were met. If the Air Force had used DOD policies or established an alternative policy that included procedures to review requirements of the new uniform prior to the start of development activities, Air Force officials may have determined that replacing combat uniforms with a non-combat uniform would leave a gap in uniform capabilities.

In addition, in developing their uniform the Air Force officials did not fully employ the key practice of using a knowledge-based approach that included the collection and use of meaningful data to determine whether a product will meet customer requirements. The Air Force tested the ABU against other service uniforms in different environments for camouflage effectiveness and conducted field tests for comfort and durability. We found that the Air Force's testing process had weaknesses, such as not testing different camouflage patterns and fabrics prior to choosing the tiger-stripe pattern, and using test results of a desert pattern in a woodland area. Also, officials chose not to implement all of the testing recommendations from the Air Force's Air Warfare Center, including one recommendation to reduce the heat build-up from the uniform.

During the development of the uniform, the Air Force conducted surveys of personnel to determine their uniform design preferences. Then, according to Air Force officials and documents, the Chief of Staff directed the Clothing Office to use a tiger-striped camouflage pattern in a uniform for all environments with colors complementing the Army's universal camouflage uniform, and to use one fabric weight for the trousers and the blouses worn in hot and cold climates. In contrast, the Marine Corp's knowledge-based approach included testing and evaluation of multiple camouflage patterns and colors from which they selected two top performing patterns. As a result, the Marine Corps produced two prototypes for extensive field testing and evaluation. Using this information, the Marine Corps was able to make knowledgeable decisions to select the best prototype and to make improvements in the design prior to production. The Marine Corps selected the same twill fabric weave that the Air Force selected for the ABU, but the Marine Corps decided to use a lighter weight fabric than the Air Force did for the uniform jacket as a way to prevent heat buildup.

In 2005, the Air Force Uniform Board sought testing of the ABU to assess the uniform's suitability for use in a combat environment and whether a second version of the uniform was needed. The Air Warfare Center produced a test plan, which included the overall test methodology and measures of uniform effectiveness and performance for concealment and comfort.

In October 2006, the Air Warfare Center issued a report on its testing of the combat effectiveness of the ABU. The report concluded that the ABU camouflage performed well in most environments—never ranking lower than third among the six uniforms in different environments. However, the report also concluded that the ABU was not an effective combat uniform due to trouser fit, heat buildup, and other concerns.

Regarding camouflage effectiveness, the Air Force compared the ABU performance to five fielded uniforms: Army Combat Uniform, Marine Corps desert and woodland uniforms, and Army Battle Dress (woodland) and Desert Camouflage uniforms. However, four of the five uniforms were environment-specific uniforms not intended for a number of settings for which they were tested. Specifically, in a tropical forest environment, the Air Force tests showed that the DCU and Marine Corp desert uniforms performed worst, and were ranked 5th and 6th respectively out of six uniforms tested. Similarly, in a desert scrub environment, the Air Force tests showed that the BDU woodland and Marine Corps woodland performed worst, ranking 5th and 6th respectively among six uniforms tested. Our analysis shows that the Air Force used camouflage test results from settings other than the ones for which they were developed, which raises questions about the meaningfulness of the report's conclusion that the ABU camouflage performed well in most environments. In 11 of 19 tests, Air Force observers rated the ABU as marginal or unsatisfactory for concealment 58 percent of the time.[27]

Additionally, the report recommended some design changes to improve fit and comfort and to improve the ABU's overall effectiveness for combat use. As a result, the Air Force incorporated some changes into the final production design, such as relocating pocket drain holes and redesigning the trouser crotch, but did not address other recommendations like the heat buildup.[28] In response, the Clothing Office noted that the original direction for the development of the ABU was for non-combat use rather than as a combat uniform or as a camouflage-effective garment.

At the conclusion of our field work, we learned that the Air Force had begun replacing the ABU with a lighter weight version to address the long standing complaints by personnel about the heat buildup issue. According to Air Force officials, the replacement ABU in a lighter weight fabric will be used by home base and deployed personnel with the exception of those serving in Afghanistan, where the Army OCP uniform will continue to be used. If Air Force officials had expanded the knowledge-based approach for selecting a uniform—such as by ordering extensive testing and evaluation of varying fabric weights for comfortable wear to support the decision process—the service may have avoided the need to replace uniforms with a lighter weight fabric.

In 2010, Air Force Central Command decided that it would be safer for personnel serving in Afghanistan to wear the Army's flame resistant OCP uniform rather than the ABU or its flame resistant uniform. Air Force Central Command determined that the ABU's camouflage contrasted with the Army's camouflage, increasing the risk of personnel standing out to enemy forces when Army and Air Force personnel were in a joint operating environment.

---

[27]We excluded 2 of 22 tests because no data was collected, and excluded another test that used subjective data.

[28]The Air Force allowed personnel to remove interior pockets in the ABU shirt to address the heat buildup issue. The Air Force web site states that to address the heat issue some personnel may choose to cut the interior pockets out of the garment, as long as it does not change the outer appearance of the uniform.

Military Services' Fragmented Approach to Developing Uniforms Has Resulted in Inconsistent Protection for Service Members and No Collaboration to Reduce Costs

The military services' fragmented approach to developing uniforms, without any joint criteria for meeting combat requirements, has not ensured that the resulting uniforms provide equivalent levels of performance and protection for service members, and the services have not collaborated to reduce the costs for uniforms in inventory. DOD has reported to the congressional defense committees on planned steps to develop joint criteria for future ground combat uniforms, but it has not met the statutory requirement to establish joint criteria. Additionally, there is no DOD policy to ensure that future service-specific uniforms comply with statutory policy to provide equivalent levels of performance and protection and minimize the risk to individual service members operating in the joint battle space, to the maximum extent practicable. We found that the services have experienced opportunities to potentially save millions of dollars in development costs and in initial inventory fees by partnering with another service in the introduction of new uniforms. At the time of our review, the services had no partnership agreement to reduce potential costs on the Army's new uniforms, and the Navy had decided to field its uniform before securing a partnership with the Coast Guard that may have achieved $6 million in cost savings for inventory fees.

DOD and Its Components Have Not Met the Statutory Requirement to Establish Joint Criteria for Ground Combat Uniforms

DOD and its service components have not collaborated to establish joint criteria for ground combat uniforms. A provision in the National Defense Authorization Act for Fiscal Year 2010 required the Secretaries of the military departments to establish joint criteria for future ground combat uniforms that ensures new technologies, advanced materials, and other advances in ground combat uniform design may be shared between the military services and are not precluded from being adapted for use by any military service due to service-unique proprietary arrangements.[29] The Secretaries of the military departments were to establish the joint criteria by February 22, 2011.[30] In June 2010, the Senate Committee on Armed Services directed the Secretary of Defense to report by August 2010 on the steps that DOD took and planned to take to implement the requirement for joint criteria, including the steps the Secretaries of the

---

[29] See Pub. L. No. 111-84, § 352(d).

[30] See id. The provision required the establishment of joint criteria no later than 270 days from the date of our report on ground combat uniforms required by section 352(c). We fulfilled the requirement with a report submitted to the congressional defense committees on April 26, 2010, but the report was published on May 28, 2010 as GAO-10-669R.

military departments took or would take—in conjunction with the Joint Staff and combatant commands—to update their ground combat uniform standards and develop operational performance criteria for camouflage.[31] DOD issued a report to congressional committees in February 2012 on the steps it planned to take to establish joint criteria for ground combat uniforms, but it has not yet met the statutory requirement to develop joint criteria.

The Joint Clothing and Textiles Governance Board, established in 2008, is the forum the military departments are using to establish joint criteria for the performance of camouflage uniforms. The governance board was established by DOD to ensure collaboration and DOD-wide integration of clothing and textile activities, such as uniforms.[32] The DOD instruction on clothing and textiles made the Director of the Defense Logistics Agency responsible for establishing and chairing the board. According to governance board officials, a working group of the governance board met in 2010 to begin discussions on the joint criteria. The working group includes representatives from the Office of the Secretary of Defense, the Joint Staff, and all the military services. However, the group's leadership did not meet the February 2011 deadline for issuing joint criteria because, according to members of the Joint Clothing and Textiles Governance Board, members of the working group were unable to obtain consensus. Our prior work has concluded that successful interagency collaboration, such as among the military services and defense agencies, requires commitment by senior officials to articulate their agreements in formal documents, such as a memorandum of understanding or interagency guidance.[33] Without high-level commitment from the Office of the Secretary of Defense, the Director of DLA may be unable to promote effective interagency cooperation and collaboration among the members of the Joint Clothing and Textiles Governance Board and ensure DOD-wide integration of clothing and textiles activities.

---

[31] See S. Rep. No. 111-201, at 117 (2010) (accompanying S. 3454, a proposed bill for the National Defense Authorization Act for Fiscal Year 2011).

[32] See DOD Instruction 4140.63, *Management of DOD Clothing and Textiles (Class II)*, encl. 2, para. 3(a) (Aug. 5, 2008).

[33] GAO, Defense Infrastructure: *High Level Leadership Needed to Help Communities Address Challenges Caused by DOD-Related Growth*, GAO-08-665 (Washington, D.C.: June 17, 2008).

Moreover, in February 2012, Joint Clothing and Textiles Governance Board officials told us that competing demands to address logistics efficiency initiatives also delayed the development of the criteria. In its February 2012 response to the congressional committees, DOD acknowledged that it could do more to promote and enhance inter-service collaboration and life-cycle coordination with the Defense Logistics Agency and provided a plan to develop joint criteria.[34] Governance board officials told us that they plan to convene a new working group and complete the joint criteria by December 2012. Further, DOD reported that the governance board will identify a common set of performance characteristics to be used across the military departments. Without joint criteria on the performance of uniforms to guide activities, one or more service may develop uniforms without knowing whether its uniforms include the newest technology, the newest materials or designs, and meet an acceptable level of performance.

Furthermore, the DOD instruction on clothing and textiles also made the Director of the Defense Logistics Agency—as chairman of the governance board—responsible for overseeing the development of a charter to outline the board's roles and responsibilities.[35] However, the charter has not been completed. An official told us that the charter has been drafted and continues to be under review by members. According to board officials, the governance board has met twice and the officials believe that the board's progress is not impeded by the lack of a signed charter. However, almost four years after the board was created, DOD has not defined the board's role. Until the board has a charter outlining its authorities, the department may continue to experience difficulty in establishing joint criteria for future ground combat uniforms.

---

[34]DOD, *Report on Requirements for Standard Ground Combat Uniforms* (Washington, D.C.:, February 2012).

[35]*See* DOD Instruction 4140.63, *Management of DOD Clothing and Textiles (Class II)*, encl. 2, para. 3(a) (Aug. 5, 2008).

DOD and Its Components Have Not Developed a Policy to Ensure That Service-Specific Uniforms Provide Equivalent Levels of Protection and Have Not Collaborated to Minimize Risk

Each military department has developed its own standards for combat uniforms, and DOD does not have a policy to ensure that the services' fragmented uniform programs comply with statutory policy to provide equivalent levels of performance and protection and minimize the risk to individual service members operating in the joint battle space, to the maximum extent practicable. The National Defense Authorization Act for Fiscal Year 2010 established policy that the design and fielding of future ground combat uniforms may uniquely reflect the identity of the individual services as long as the uniforms, to the maximum extent practicable, provide equivalent levels of performance and protection for members commensurate with their respective assigned combat missions and minimize the risk to the individual soldier, sailor, airman, or marine operating in the joint battle space, among other things.[36] Separately, under DOD's instruction on clothing and textile management, the Under Secretary of Defense for Acquisition, Technology, and Logistics is responsible for the development of DOD policy and implementing guidance on all matters relating to the clothing and textiles supply chain.[37]

We found that the services have not collaborated on uniform development, and have not ensured that their current service-unique uniforms provide equivalent levels of performance and protection and minimize risk to individual service members operating in the joint battle space. DOD and the Joint Staff have described the modern-day battlefield as a place with no clearly defined front lines or safer rear area where combat support operations are performed.[38] In such an environment, service members wearing uniforms consisting of different camouflage may be exposed to different levels of risk. For example, the Air Force requires personnel in Afghanistan to wear a camouflage uniform that best protects them and enables them to blend with other service members with whom they operate to minimize risk. However, the Navy requires some personnel in the desert environment to wear different camouflage uniforms, potentially exposing them to increased risk.

---

[36] See Pub. L. No. 111-84, § 352(a).

[37] Department of Defense Instruction 4140.63, *Management of DOD Clothing and Textiles (Class II)*, encl. 3, para. 1 (Aug. 5, 2008).

[38] DOD, *Report to Congress on the Review of Laws, Policies and Regulations Restricting the Service of Female Members in the U.S. Armed Forces* (Washington, D.C.:, February 2012).

In September 2010, Air Force Central Command decided to enhance the level of protection of personnel serving in Afghanistan by directing personnel to wear the Army's OCP uniform (where available) rather than the Air Force's existing ABU and flame-resistant uniform. According to Air Force officials, this action was taken to reduce the risk of any personnel standing out in the joint operating environment. Conversely, the Navy limited the use of its Type II desert uniform in desert environments. In a 2009 administrative message, the Navy stated that the Type II desert and Type III woodland uniforms would increase the probability of mission success and survivability in combat and irregular warfare operations.[39] However, the Navy also indicated that only Naval Special Warfare personnel and sailors assigned to or directly supporting Naval Special Warfare units would be authorized to wear the Type II desert uniform. Although the Navy later revised its guidance on wear of the Type II desert and Type III woodland uniforms,[40] this restriction and its focus on personnel from or supporting Naval Special Warfare units largely remained. As a result of the policy, some Navy units, such as construction and intelligence units, were issued the woodland Type III uniforms to wear in desert environments.

In June 2010, the Senate Committee on Armed Services expressed concern about the Navy's restricted use of the uniform among its personnel.[41] In hearings before the Subcommittee on Readiness and Management Support in April 2010, the Assistant Commandant of the Marine Corps testified that Marine Corps and Navy discussions prompted the Navy's policy to restrict the use of its Type II desert combat uniform. When the Marine Corps first learned that the new Navy uniform looked very similar to the Marine Corps' combat uniform, the Assistant Commandant testified, the Marine Corps suggested the selection of a Navy pattern that was different enough to distinguish it from the uniform worn by the Marines. However, the Assistant Commandant testified, the Marine Corps Commandant and the Chief of Naval Operations later reached an agreement that forward-deployed Navy SEALS and similar

---

[39]Chief of Naval Operations, NAVADMIN 374-09, *Navy Working Uniform Type II and III* (Dec. 29, 2009).

[40]Chief of Naval Operations, NAVADMIN 259-11, *Navy* Working *Uniform Type I, II, and III, Camouflage Utility Uniforms* (Aug. 30, 2011). The Navy guidance was revised, in part, to allow U.S. Coast Guard personnel to wear Navy uniforms under certain conditions.

[41]*See* S. Rep. No. 111-201, at 117 (2010).

personnel could use the Type II desert uniform. The effect of the agreement, however, is that it does not allow other Navy ground support units to wear the Type II uniform. According to Navy officials, the Navy did not approve a waiver requested by the Commander of the Navy Expeditionary Combat Command to allow expeditionary sailors, not directly supporting Naval Special Warfare, to wear the desert uniform in a desert environment. The Navy's restriction on the use of its Type II desert uniform appears inconsistent with the department's prevailing view of the modern-day battlefield.

DOD has not developed a policy to ensure that future service-specific uniforms provide equivalent levels of performance and protection and minimize risk to the individual operating in the joint battle space. In its February 2012 response to congressional committees about ground combat uniforms, DOD reported on the Joint Clothing and Textiles Governance Board's activities to improve performance of uniforms. As part of its effort to establish joint criteria and standardize uniforms, the Joint Clothing and Textiles Governance Board plans to identify a common set of performance characteristics. The governance board intends for the performance characteristics to be used across the military departments to develop and field the most effective camouflage uniforms and personal protective gear to ensure maximum protection for the troops. However, common performance characteristics alone may not fully minimize risk without also considering the effects of combining different uniforms in the same battle space. Without a policy to ensure that services develop and field uniforms with equivalent performance and protection, the services could fall short of offering equivalent protection for all service members, and DOD could expose even those service members wearing the most effective camouflage available to unnecessary risks.

Military Services Have Not Fully Explored Partnership Opportunities to Reduce Inventory Costs

Although the statutory policy permits the services to pursue unique uniform designs, the services' fragmented approach to developing camouflage uniforms has resulted in numerous inventories of similar uniforms at increased cost to the supply chain. As presented earlier in this report, each service now has its own set of camouflaged uniforms—the Army and Air Force with their universal camouflage ACU, OCP and ABU uniforms, and the Marine Corps and Navy with their environment-specific MARPAT and Type I and II woodland and desert camouflage uniforms. In addition, each service has developed a separate flame resistant version of its uniforms. Maintaining inventory levels of reserve and contingency stock for multiple versions of camouflage uniforms, in aggregate, requires a larger total inventory of uniforms than would be necessary to support a product line with fewer uniform versions, and the services have not taken advantage of opportunities to reduce costs through partnering on inventory management or by collaborating to achieve greater standardization among their various camouflage uniform versions.

Under DOD's supply chain regulation on materiel management, DOD components are encouraged, but not required, to standardize basic materials and accessories and to standardize uniforms and other clothing items when possible to reduce costs.[42] However, according to DLA officials, none of the services has partnered on combat uniforms since they began separately replacing the BDU and DCU beginning in 2002. Instead, each of the services generally went its own way in developing or adopting service-specific camouflage uniforms. For example, the goals for the Marine Corps' uniform development program included providing Marines with a unique combat uniform, the Air Force wanted a utility uniform with a distinctively Air Force look, the Navy's goals were to adopt a set of uniforms that reflected the requirements of a 21st century Navy and its naval heritage, and the Army wanted a new uniform that would be more widely accepted by its soldiers than the BDU. The services' fragmented approaches to uniform development began with the Marine Corps in 2002 and continued for other services until the Navy was the last service to replace the BDU in 2011 with camouflage uniforms developed for naval special forces. During our review, we found that the services collectively have spent approximately $12.5 million for uniform development since 2000 or an average of $2.1 million for each of the six development programs that we reviewed.

In addition, DOD's supply chain regulation states that any desired distinctiveness for clothing items should be accomplished by methods such as using separate items of insignia and patches. However, two services—the Marine Corps and the Navy—have printed their service logos on the camouflage-patterned fabric during the manufacturing process. We have previously reported that the Marine Corps patents on elements of the uniform do not preclude another service from adopting the Marine Corps' uniform. However, given the prevailing military service culture that places a high value on having distinctive and unique combat uniforms, the printing of a service's logo on a uniform's fabric might make

---

[42]See Department of Defense Regulation 4140.1-R, *DOD Supply Chain Materiel Management Regulation*, chapter 8 (May 23, 2003).

it difficult for another service to adopt the uniform for temporary mission needs or as a permanent replacement unless the printed logo was removed. Conversely, the Army and the Air Force have not found it necessary to print their service logos on their combat uniforms. The Army, for example, has been open in allowing members of another service to wear its uniform to meet mission needs.

We also found that the services have not reduced costs by collaborating to eliminate inventory fees for new uniforms. When the military services introduce a new item, the Defense Logistics Agency imposes an initial inventory fee if the cost of the new item is greater than 10 percent of the cost of the item being replaced and if the item is introduced into inventory by only one DOD component.[43] The inventory fee covers the cost of acquiring initial inventory, according to Defense Logistics Agency officials, and includes the first four months of inventory, a three-month safety level, and the cost of the remaining uniforms in inventory being replaced.[44] To encourage the services to reduce costs by standardizing materials and eliminating duplication, according to the Defense Logistics Agency, Troop Support office, officials will waive the initial inventory fee if two or more services agree to jointly introduce the item into their inventories.

Two military services, the Army and the Navy, have recently experienced opportunities to potentially save tens of millions of dollars in initial inventory fees by partnering with another service in the introduction of new uniforms. The Army is currently testing camouflage patterns to support the development of new camouflage uniforms for service-wide use and has estimated that the service could avoid initial inventory fees of as much as $82 million by partnering with another service or services. However, during our review none of the services had reached an agreement to partner with the Army. According to PEO Soldier officials, they have coordinated with the other services by hosting an Integrated Product Team to obtain input on their development activities and included

---

[43]For new clothing with a forecasted total annual demand value exceeding $100,000, DOD policy provides that the initial investment and acquisition of inventory levels to satisfy demands up to the effective date of supply is the financial responsibility of the requesting component. Officials of the Defense Logistics Agency's Troop Support office stated that their interpretation of the policy is that items with a value of 10 percent greater than the item being replaced will include the initial inventory fee.

[44]According to Defense Logistics Agency officials, the initial inventory fee is based on a calculation of the monthly demand, the speed of fielding, and the cost of the new uniforms.

Marine Corps and Navy camouflage uniforms in the baseline testing to evaluate new camouflage patterns. The Air Force is monitoring the Army's activities and Air Force officials stated that they are considering using the new uniforms if the uniforms meet their requirements. Nevertheless, we found that Army officials have not reached an agreement with the Air Force or other services to partner on the joint introduction of its uniforms to achieve cost savings if the initial inventory fee applies. If the Army does not partner with at least one service on the introduction of its new uniforms, it will miss an opportunity to eliminate the initial inventory fee cost, decrease the life-cycle costs of its uniforms, and may duplicate effort if the Air Force or another service later decides to independently develop a new uniform.

The Navy, as part of its acquisition planning in the spring of 2011, estimated potential cost savings of about $6 million in its initial inventory fees if it partnered with another service in the introduction of its Type II desert and Type III woodland uniforms. In March 2011, the Coast Guard requested approval from the Navy, Naval Special Warfare Command, and U.S. Special Operations Command to use the camouflage uniforms for maritime, counter-terrorism, and security missions. The Coast Guard request stated that the uniform partnership would promote the active relationship between the Coast Guard and the Navy and provide interoperability and cooperation in the joint maritime environment. In August 2011, the Navy revised guidance on the wear of its uniforms, permitting the Coast Guard to use its Type II desert uniform for Coast Guard personnel assigned to or directly supporting Naval Special Warfare, and it approved use of the Type III woodland uniforms for all other Coast Guard personnel.[45] Nevertheless, Navy officials decided to field the uniform before establishing a formal partnership with the Coast Guard. As a result, the Navy incurred $6 million in inventory fees, thereby increasing the overall life-cycle cost of the uniforms.

In the absence of DOD requirements that the services collaborate to standardize the development and introduction of camouflage uniforms, the services may continue to miss opportunities to increase efficiencies and forego tens of millions of dollars in cost savings.

---

[45]See Chief of Naval Operations, NAVADMIN 259-11, Navy Working Uniform Type I, II, and III, Camouflage Utility Uniforms (Aug. 30, 2011).

Conclusions

In the past 10 years, each of the military services independently introduced at least one service-specific camouflage uniform, and two services' uniforms did not meet requirements and needed to be replaced. DOD has provided the services with guidance for acquisitions through its 5000-series instruction, but all services did not follow that guidance because they determined it was not applicable to their development and acquisition of uniforms or they did not apply the guidance in a manner that would ensure effective outcomes. In addition, DOD did not clarify the appropriate use of this or other guidance when developing combat uniforms, resulting in varying, fragmented procedures that did not consistently produce effective camouflage uniforms. By not following two key practices for a decision-making process that can produce successful outcomes, military services developed uniforms that did not meet specific mission requirements. DOD has provided some additional clarity in the 2008 instruction on the management of clothing and textiles, but the military services may continue to vary in their application and use of acquisition guidance. With additional clarity from DOD on the consistent use of policies and procedures and a knowledge-based approach, the services could increase their assurance of having a disciplined process that is capable of developing uniforms that meet warfighter requirements.

Additionally, the military services have fragmented approaches to developing uniforms that do not rely on joint criteria for meeting combat requirements, do not ensure that the resulting uniforms provide equivalent levels of performance and protection, and do not lead to collaboration to reduce the costs for uniforms in inventory. Without a high-level commitment from the Office of the Secretary of Defense, the Director of the Defense Logistics Agency may be unable to promote effective interagency cooperation and collaboration among the members of the Joint Clothing and Textiles Governance Board. If the services developed and used joint criteria for meeting combat requirements, service officials could increase assurance that their new uniforms include the newest technology and the newest materials or designs, and meet an acceptable level of performance. Also, by completing the board's charter to outline the board's roles and responsibilities, the board could increase the likelihood that its members would establish the joint criteria for uniforms required by statute in 2009. The services have not established a means to assess and ensure that future uniforms will fulfill statutory policy regarding service-unique uniforms and, as a result, may not be able to ensure that future ground combat uniforms provide all service members with equivalent levels of protection and performance or minimize risks while operating in the joint battle space. Finally, the services' fragmented approach to uniform development has resulted in the services not standardizing camouflage uniforms, not collaborating or partnering on inventory fees to reduce development and inventory costs, and potentially not saving on overall procurement costs. Standardizing the development of camouflage uniforms and partnering to share inventory fees could increase efficiency in uniform development programs and potentially save DOD tens of millions of dollars over the life cycles of the services' combat utility uniforms.

Recommendations for Executive Action

We recommend that the Secretary of Defense take the following four actions:

- To better ensure camouflage uniforms being developed by the military services meet mission requirements, direct the Under Secretary of Defense for Acquisition, Technology, and Logistics to ensure that the services have and consistently use clear policies and procedures and a knowledge-based approach to produce successful outcomes.

- To facilitate the department's ability to meet the statutory requirement to develop joint criteria for camouflage uniforms, direct the Secretaries of the military departments to identify and implement actions necessary to enable the Joint Clothing and Textiles Governance Board to develop and issue joint criteria for uniforms prior to the development or acquisition of any new camouflage uniform. These actions should include efforts to ensure the completion of the Joint Clothing and Textiles Governance Board's charter outlining the roles, responsibilities, and authorities of the board, and establishing a timeline for developing joint standards.

- To address the statutory policy related to camouflage uniforms, direct the Under Secretary of Defense for Acquisition, Technology, and Logistics to develop a policy and establish a timeframe to ensure that future service-specific uniforms provide equivalent levels of performance and protection, and minimize risk to service members operating in the joint battle space.

- To take advantage of potential efficiencies and cost savings when introducing new uniforms, direct the Secretaries of the military departments to actively pursue partnerships for the joint development and use of uniforms to minimize fragmentation in the development of uniforms, and to seek to reduce inventory and overall procurement costs.

Agency Comments and Our Evaluation

We provided a draft of this report to DOD for comment. In written comments, reprinted in their entirety in appendix III, DOD concurred with our recommendations. DOD also provided technical comments, which we have incorporated, as appropriate. In response to our recommendations, DOD stated that steps will be taken to improve the use of policy and procedures during development of uniforms, to address statutory requirements and policy, and take advantage of potential efficiencies and cost savings.

DOD concurred with our recommendation that the Secretary of Defense direct the Under Secretary of Defense for Acquisition, Technology, and Logistics to ensure that the services have, and consistently use, clear policies and procedures and a knowledge-based approach to produce successful outcomes. DOD said that (USD) AT&L will place additional emphasis on the importance of following guidance related to the Defense Acquisition System and the Joint Capabilities Integration and Development System through oversight by the Joint Clothing and Textiles Governance Board. If DOD completes the Joint Clothing and Textiles Government Board charter clearly outlining the roles, responsibilities, and authorities of the Board to include oversight of the services' uniform development process, then the action proposed by the department may satisfy the intent of the recommendation. However, DOD did not specifically identify how the Joint Clothing and Textiles Governance Board plans to provide consistent, long-term oversight to ensure the military services use policies and procedures to guide their development activities in the future. As we discuss in our report, without additional guidance from DOD on the use of clear policies and procedures for a knowledge-based approach to developing effective uniforms, some services may continue to lack assurance that they have a disciplined process that is capable of delivering uniforms that meet warfighter requirements.

DOD concurred with our recommendation that the Secretary of Defense direct the Secretaries of the military departments to identify and implement actions necessary to enable the Joint Clothing and Textiles Governance Board to develop and issue joint criteria for uniforms prior to the development or acquisition of any new camouflage uniform and establishing a timeline for developing joint standards. One important action includes the completion of the Board's charter outlining the roles, responsibilities, and authorities of the board. DOD stated that the military departments participate in the Joint Clothing and Textiles Governance Board's efforts to develop joint criteria for camouflage uniforms by providing appropriate research and development and functional expertise. DOD stated that draft joint criteria for camouflage uniforms have been developed and are going through the DOD approval process, which DOD estimated will be completed in the 2nd quarter of Fiscal Year 2013. Finally, DOD stated that once approved, the joint criteria will be used prior to the development or acquisition of new camouflage uniforms. While we are encouraged to learn that DOD has draft joint criteria moving through the approval process, the development of the joint criteria has been an ongoing effort for several years—initially to be completed by February 2011, then in December 2012, according to DOD's status report to congressional committees, and now no later than March 2013, in response to our recommendation. Because of the difficulties the department has experienced in developing and approving joint criteria, our recommendation called for the completion of the Joint Clothing and Textiles Governance Board's charter as a specific action that DOD should take to facilitate the department's ability to meet the statutory requirement to develop joint criteria for future ground combat uniforms. DOD, however, did not address completion of the Board's charter in its comments. We continue to believe that completion of the charter to clearly outline the roles, responsibilities, and authorities of the Board would facilitate military department approval of meaningful joint criteria. Further, we believe that completion of the Board's charter will be critical in ensuring that the Board can assist DOD in 1) carrying out the oversight of service uniform development actions and 2) providing additional oversight and encouraging active partnerships for joint development and use of uniforms, particularly since DOD has identified the Board as an essential actor in carrying out three of our four recommendations.

DOD concurred with our recommendation that the Under Secretary of Defense for Acquisition, Technology, and Logistics develop a policy and establish a timeframe to ensure that future service-specific uniforms provide equivalent levels of performance and protection, and minimize risk to service members operating in the joint battlespace. DOD said that the USD (AT&L) will disseminate policy guidance to the military departments that will include direction for using joint criteria and ensuring equivalent levels of performance and protection by the 3rd quarter of Fiscal Year 2013. If fully implemented, we believe this action would satisfy our recommendation.

DOD concurred with our recommendation that the Secretaries of the military departments actively pursue partnerships for the joint development and use of uniforms to minimize fragmentation in the development of uniforms, and to seek to reduce inventory and overall procurement costs. DOD stated that it will use the Joint Clothing and Textiles Governance Board and the Cross-Service Warfighter Equipment

Board to provide additional oversight and further pursue active partnerships for joint development and use of uniforms. We believe these actions, if fully implemented, would satisfy our recommendation.

We are sending copies of this report to appropriate congressional committees, the Secretary of Defense, the Under Secretary of Defense for Acquisition, Technology, and Logistics; the Secretaries of the Air Force, Army, and Navy, the Commandant of the Marine Corps, and other interested parties. In addition, the report will be available at no charge on the GAO website at http://www.gao.gov.

If you or your staff has any questions concerning this report, please contact me at (202) 512-5431 or russellc@gao.gov. Contact points for our Offices of Congressional Relations and Public Affairs may be found on the last page of this report. Key contributors to this report are listed in appendix IV.

Cary B. Russell,
Acting Director,
Defense Capabilities and Management

Appendix I: Scope and Methodology

To determine the extent to which Department of Defense (DOD) guidance provides a consistent decision process to ensure that new camouflage uniforms meet operational requirements, we reviewed key guidance and interviewed relevant DOD and military service officials. We collected and reviewed the DOD's and services' regulations, instructions, policies, procedures, and other guidance that the services used to structure their decision processes on the development and acquisition of their camouflage uniforms. We assessed the decision processes based on their use of DOD's 5000-series acquisition guidance, military department implementing guidance, or other guidance, and OMB's acquisition guidance and GAO's framework for assessing acquisition functions. We assessed whether three services—the Marine Corps, Army and Air Force—followed the two key elements that GAO has determined are key practices for a decision process that produces successful outcomes, and to what extent each service developed uniforms that met requirements. We visited the Army, Marine Corps, Air Force, and Navy offices responsible for managing the development or acquisition of their camouflage uniforms and gathered data and reports that the services used to support their decisions. We interviewed military service officials responsible for the management of uniform development and acquisition policy and the Office of the Under Secretary of Defense for Acquisition, Technology, and Logistics about the flexibility of DOD's 5000-series guidance and how the services used this guidance in their development activities. To determine whether the services' uniforms met requirements, we collected data and interviewed service officials to determine if the new uniforms have been replaced to meet operational needs.

To determine the extent to which the services have used a joint approach to develop criteria, ensure equivalent protection and manage costs, we reviewed the DOD guidance, the requirement of the National Defense Authorization Act for Fiscal Year 2010 that the military departments establish joint criteria for future ground combat uniforms, and policy established by the act permitting the design and fielding of service-unique, future ground combat uniforms so long as they, to the maximum extent practicable, provide equivalent levels of performance and protection to all service members commensurate with their assigned combat missions and minimize the risk to the individual service members operating in the joint battle space, among other things.[1] We collected data

---

[1] See Pub. L. No. 111-84, § 352(a), (d).

and interviewed relevant officials from the four military services and officials with the Joint Clothing and Textiles Governance Board from the Office of the Under Secretary of Defense for Acquisition, Technology, and Logistics and the Defense Logistics Agency to determine if the services are using a joint approach to address the requirement and policy and if they are being met. Specifically, we interviewed governance board officials and reviewed documents related to the board's efforts and plans to develop joint criteria and collect a set of common uniform characteristics to support development of uniforms and protective gear. Finally, to determine how the services jointly seek to reduce costs in the acquisition of uniforms, we gathered data from the Navy and Army on the estimated cost to introduce their new camouflage uniforms into inventory. We reviewed DOD's supply chain materiel management regulation and other guidance from the Defense Logistics Agency, Troop Support office on initial inventory fees and how the agency provides the services a reduced initial inventory fee if a service partners with one or more service. To assess the reliability of the cost data, we interviewed Navy and Army officials to understand how the initial inventory fee was determined. The Defense Logistics Agency confirmed the cost of the Navy's initial inventory fee. To verify the Army's estimate, we obtained data from the Defense Logistics Agency, Troop Support office on monthly demand for uniforms and created our own cost estimate. To ensure that the computer-generated data from the Defense Logistics Agency, Troop Support office is reliable, we collected information about the Enterprise Business System and the Standard Materiel Management System and interviewed officials who manage the system. We determined that the data from the Defense Logistics Agency, Troop Support office, the Navy, and the Army were sufficiently reliable for the purpose of our engagement.

We conducted this performance audit from September 2010 to September 2012 in accordance with generally accepted government auditing standards. These standards require that we plan and perform the audit to obtain sufficient, appropriate evidence to provide a reasonable basis for our findings and conclusions based on our audit objectives. We believe that the evidence obtained provides a reasonable basis for our findings and conclusions based on our audit objectives.

Appendix II: Flame Resistant Ground Combat Uniforms

Since 2006, each service has developed or adopted flame-resistant uniforms in response to urgent warfighter needs. See figure 2 for additional information about the uniforms. Prior to Operation Enduring Freedom and Operation Iraqi Freedom, DOD personnel with flame resistant uniforms were mainly aviators, fuel handlers, and combat-vehicle crewmen. These personnel required flame resistant uniforms because of their potential exposure to fire or other thermal energy. With the growing prevalence of the Improvised Explosive Device (IED) threat, all ground forces serving in Iraq and Afghanistan have been exposed to the possibility of fire-related injuries. As the threat from IEDs emerged and continues today, the services have developed flame resistant uniform capabilities to protect the warfighter.

Figure 2: Services' Flame Resistant Uniforms, Dates of Initiation, and Development Costs

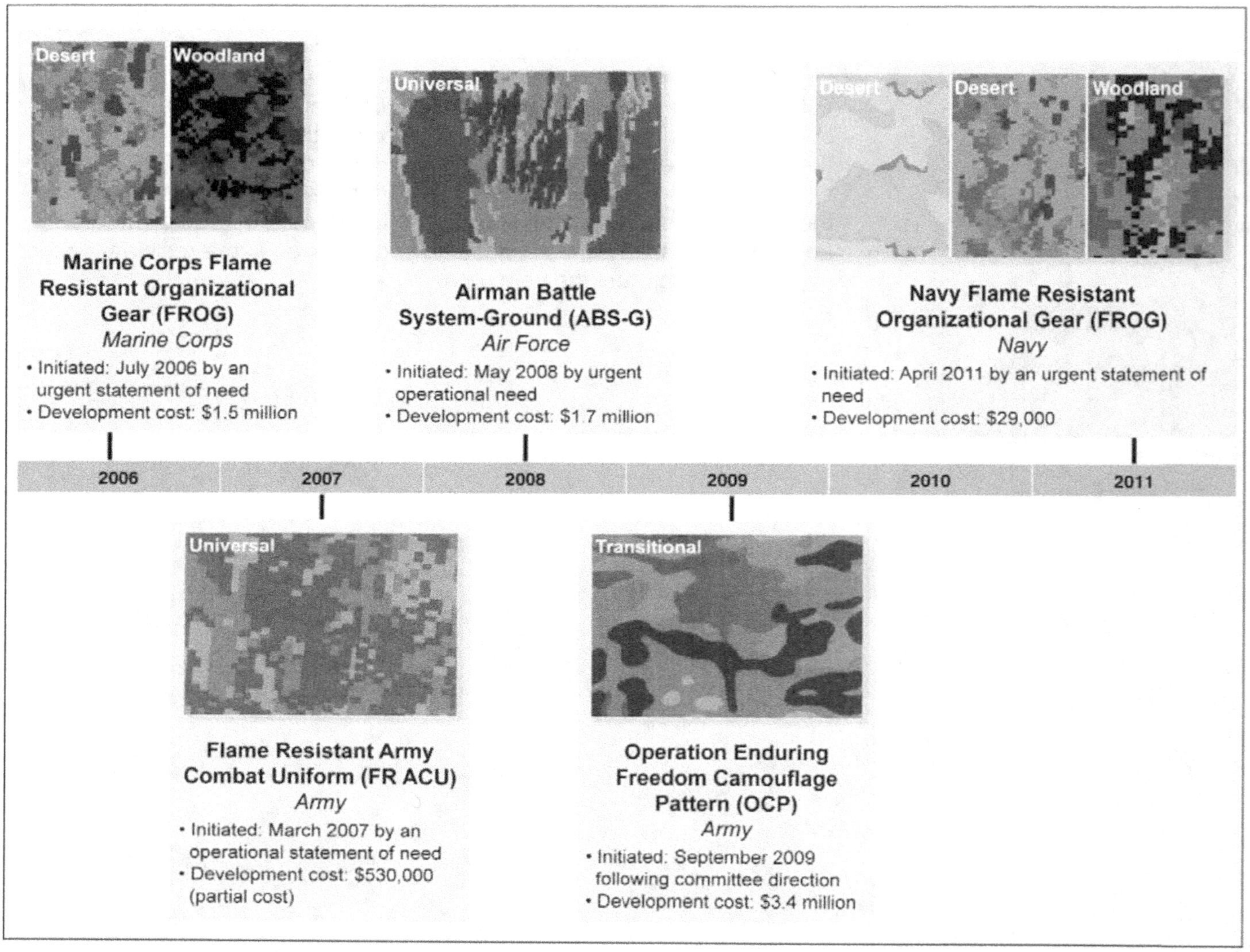
Desert
Woodland
Marine Corps Flame Resistant Organizational Gear (FROG)
Marine Corps
• Initiated: July 2006 by an urgent statement of need
• Development cost: $1.5 million
Universal
Airman Battle System-Ground (ABS-G)
Air Force
• Initiated: May 2008 by urgent operational need
• Development cost: $1.7 million
Desert
Desert
Woodland
Navy Flame Resistant Organizational Gear (FROG)
Navy
• Initiated: April 2011 by an urgent statement of need
• Development cost: $29,000
2006
2007
2008
2009
2010
2011
Universal
Flame Resistant Army Combat Uniform (FR ACU)
Army
• Initiated: March 2007 by an operational statement of need
• Development cost: $530,000 (partial cost)
Transitional
Operation Enduring Freedom Camouflage Pattern (OCP)
Army
• Initiated: September 2009 following committee direction
• Development cost: $3.4 million

Source: DOD.

The Marine Corps developed its Flame Resistant Organizational Gear (FROG) in response to a July 2006 Urgent Statement of Need to increase protection against flash flame IED events in Central Command's area of responsibility. The Urgent Statement of Need requested burn protection for the hands, face, and neck. After extensive testing, the Marine Corps determined that in addition to providing a base layer of protection, the service also needed to provide an outer layer of protection. The Marine Corps conducted testing of flame-resistant fabrics in January and February of 2007 and selected the *TenCate Defender™ M* fabric for its flame-resistant uniforms. The Marine Corps spent about $1.5 million in the development of the FROG through Fiscal Year 2008. The service began fielding FROG items in February 2007 to all deployed and deploying Marines.

The Army's Flame Resistant Army Combat Uniform (FR ACU) was developed in response to two Operational Need Statements requiring flame protection clothing capabilities to support operations in Central Command's area of responsibility due to greater threats of IEDs with enhanced accelerants throughout the theater. In August 2006, the Army received an Operational Need Statement from Multi-National Corps Iraq which called for an increase in the number of flame-resistant uniforms already available to be used by soldiers to protect against increased burn injuries occurring from IED attacks. The Operational Need Statement was met by issuing Nomex® Combat Vehicle Crewman's uniforms and Nomex® Combat Vehicle Crewman's balaclavas for those soldiers deployed in support of Operations Iraqi Freedom and Operation Enduring Freedom. In addition, as part of its response, the Army tested flame-resistant fabrics in 2006 for future uniforms. In March 2007, an Operational Needs Statement was submitted by United States Army Central requesting flame-resistant uniforms to enhance survivability while conducting missions. The Army developed its FR ACU using the same flame-resistant fabric, *TenCate Defender™ M*, identified in its 2006 testing and as the Marine Corps' FROG. The Army did not provide the total cost of the development of the FR ACU, but did provide PEO Soldier's research and development costs of about $530,000. The Army began fielding the FR ACU to soldiers in late 2007.

In response to direction from a June 2009 conference committee that DOD take immediate action to provide personnel deployed to Afghanistan with a camouflage pattern that is suited to the environment of Afghanistan,[1] the Army developed the Operation Enduring Freedom Camouflage Pattern (OCP). The OCP uniform provides increased camouflage protection to soldiers operating in Afghanistan's diverse

---

[1]*See* H.R. Rep. No. 111-151, at 86 (2009) (Conf. Rep., accompanying the Supplemental Appropriations Act, 2009).

environments and is printed on the *TenCate Defender™ M* flame resistant fabric. The Army spent about $3.4 million through 2009 on development, began fielding the uniform in July 2010, and it is expected to be fully fielded by September 2012.

The Air Force's Airman Battle System-Ground (ABS-G) was developed in response to a May 2008 Urgent Operational Need for flame-resistant equipment to be used in ground combat and combat support environments by personnel performing non-traditional, ground-focused, or newly emerging missions for the Air Force and in support of other joint and services' staffs in Central Command's area of responsibility. The ABS-G consists of four layers of flame-resistant clothing: a base layer, core layer, an outer layer, and an extreme cold-weather layer. In 2007, the Air Force and Army conducted joint testing of flame-resistant fabrics to identify alternatives to *TenCate Defender™ M* based on concerns about the availability of flame resistant rayon given a projected increase in demand from both services. The Air Force spent about $1.7 million between 2007 and 2010 in the development of the ABS-G and began fielding it in March 2009. However, in September 2010, the Air Force changed its combat uniform wear policy to enhance the level of protection for personnel who perform ground combat missions. The updated policy authorizes personnel conducting ground combat missions beyond the perimeter of a base to wear the uniform of their assigned or aligned unit—generally the Army's OCP—and directs all other Air Force personnel deployed to Afghanistan to wear the Army's OCP uniform or the FR ACU if the OCP uniform is not available. If neither uniform is available, the policy authorizes personnel to wear the ABS-G. Air Force officials stated that the ABS-G will be transitioned out of the Air Force's inventory as soon as the production levels of the Army's flame-resistant uniforms can meet Air Force demand.

In response to an Urgent Statement of Need dated February 2011, the Navy adopted the Marine Corps' flame resistant uniform for Navy use, thereby avoiding a duplication of effort and eliminating development costs. Through the Naval Logistics Integration initiative with the Marine Corps, the Navy is leveraging the Marine Corps' flame resistant uniform and gear and adding its own Type II desert and Type III woodland camouflage patterns and the legacy Desert Camouflage Uniform patterns to the FROG uniform for use by the Navy's expeditionary ground personnel. The Marine Corps Systems Command's Program Manager for Infantry Combat Equipment (PM-ICE) is the program manager for the Navy expeditionary ground personnel's flame-resistant uniforms. The Navy spent about $29,000 for final preproduction review of the uniforms and had no additional research or development costs because it adopted the Marine Corps' flame-resistant uniform. The Navy began fielding elements of the Navy FROG in September 2011. According to an official, the Navy plans to begin fielding its FROG in the Type II desert pattern in 2012.

Appendix III: Comments from the Department of Defense

ASSISTANT SECRETARY OF DEFENSE
3500 DEFENSE PENTAGON
WASHINGTON, DC 20301-3500

LOGISTICS AND
MATERIEL READINESS

SEP 2 5 2012

Mr. Cary B. Russell
Acting Director
Defense Capabilities and Management
U.S. Government Accountability Office
441 G Street, N.W.
Washington, DC 20548

Dear Mr. Russell:

This is the Department of Defense (DoD) response to the Government Accountability Office (GAO) draft report, GAO-12-707, "WARFIGHTER SUPPORT: DoD Should Improve Development of Camouflage Uniforms and Enhance Collaboration Among the Services," dated August 22, 2012 (GAO Code 351527).

The Department concurs with the draft report recommendations that DoD improve the development of camouflage uniforms and enhance collaboration among the Services by ensuring the Military Departments: a) have and use clear policies and procedures and a knowledge-based approach; b) establish joint criteria; c) develop policy to ensure equivalent protection levels; and d) establish partnerships where applicable to help reduce costs. Detailed comments on the report recommendations are enclosed.

The Department appreciates the opportunity to comment on the draft report. Technical comments have been provided separately. For further questions concerning this report, please contact Mr. Lee Plowden, Logistics and Materiel Readiness, at 571-372-5204 or lee.plowden@osd.mil.

Sincerely,

Alan F. Estevez

Enclosure:
As stated

GAO DRAFT REPORT DATED AUGUST 22, 2012
GAO-12-707 (GAO CODE 351527)

"WARFIGHTER SUPPORT: DOD SHOULD IMPROVE DEVELOPMENT OF
CAMOUFLAGE UNIFORMS AND ENHANCE COLLABORATION AMONG
THE SERVICES"

DEPARTMENT OF DEFENSE COMMENTS
TO THE GAO RECOMMENDATIONS

RECOMMENDATION 1: GAO recommends that the Secretary of Defense take the
following action to better ensure camouflage uniforms being developed by the Military
Services meet mission requirements, direct the Under Secretary of Defense for
Acquisition, Technology, and Logistics (USD(AT&L)) to ensure that the Services have
and consistently use clear policies and procedures and a knowledge-based approach to
produce successful outcomes.

DOD RESPONSE: Concur. DoD Instruction 5000.02, "Operation of the Defense
Acquisition System," and CJCS Instruction 3170.01H, "Joint Capabilities Integration and
Development System," provide the policy and procedures necessary for the Military
Departments to produce successful outcomes. USD(AT&L) will place additional
emphasis on the importance of following these policies and procedures through oversight
by the Joint Clothing and Textile Governance Board (JCTGB).

RECOMMENDATION 2: GAO recommends that the Secretary of Defense take the
following action to facilitate the department's ability to meet the statutory requirement to
develop joint criteria for camouflage uniforms, direct the Secretaries of the Military
Departments to identify and implement actions necessary to enable the JCTGB to
develop and issue joint criteria for uniforms prior to the development or acquisition of
any new camouflage uniform. These actions should include efforts to ensure the
completion of the Joint Clothing and Textile Governance Board's charter outlining the
roles, responsibilities, and authorities of the board, and establishing a timeline for
developing joint standards.

DOD RESPONSE: Concur. The Military Departments participate in the JCTGB effort
to develop joint criteria for camouflage uniforms by providing appropriate research and
development and functional expertise. Draft joint criteria for camouflage uniforms have
been developed and are going through the DoD approval process. The estimated
completion for approval is 2nd Quarter FY 2013. After approval, the criteria will be used
prior to the development or acquisition of new camouflage uniforms.

RECOMMENDATION 3: GAO recommends that the Secretary of Defense take the
following action to facilitate the statutory policy related to camouflage uniforms, direct
the Under Secretary of Defense for Acquisition, Technology, and Logistics to develop a

2

policy and establish a timeframe to ensure that future service-specific uniforms provide equivalent levels of performance and protection, and minimize risk to service members operating in the joint battle space.

DOD RESPONSE: Concur. USD(ATL) will disseminate policy guidance to the Military Departments that will include direction for using joint criteria and ensuring equivalent levels of performance and protection. The estimated completion date is 3rd Quarter FY 2013.

RECOMMENDATION 4: GAO recommends that the Secretary of Defense take the following action to take advantage of potential efficiencies and cost savings when introducing new uniforms, direct the Secretaries of the Military Departments to actively pursue partnerships for the joint development and use of uniforms to minimize fragmentation in the development of uniforms, and to seek to reduce inventory and overall procurement costs.

DOD RESPONSE: Concur. DoD Instruction 4140.63, "Management of DOD Clothing and Textiles (Class II)," directs the Military Departments to emphasize efficiency and cost savings in uniform development. DoD will use the JCTGB and Cross-Service Warfighter Equipment Board to provide additional oversight and further pursuit of active partnerships for joint development and use of uniforms.

2

Appendix IV: GAO Contact and Staff Acknowledgments

GAO Contact	Cary Russell, Acting Director, Defense Capabilities and Management, (202) 512-5431 or russellc@gao.gov.
Staff Acknowledgments	In addition to the contact name above, key contributors to this report were Larry Junek, Assistant Director; Elizabeth Morris, Grace Coleman, Susan Ditto, James Lackey, Tobin McMurdie, Carol Petersen, Richard Powelson, Michael Shaughnessy, and Amie Steele.

GAO's Mission	The Government Accountability Office, the audit, evaluation, and investigative arm of Congress, exists to support Congress in meeting its constitutional responsibilities and to help improve the performance and accountability of the federal government for the American people. GAO examines the use of public funds; evaluates federal programs and policies; and provides analyses, recommendations, and other assistance to help Congress make informed oversight, policy, and funding decisions. GAO's commitment to good government is reflected in its core values of accountability, integrity, and reliability.
Obtaining Copies of GAO Reports and Testimony	The fastest and easiest way to obtain copies of GAO documents at no cost is through GAO's website (http://www.gao.gov). Each weekday afternoon, GAO posts on its website newly released reports, testimony, and correspondence. To have GAO e-mail you a list of newly posted products, go to http://www.gao.gov and select "E-mail Updates."
Order by Phone	The price of each GAO publication reflects GAO's actual cost of production and distribution and depends on the number of pages in the publication and whether the publication is printed in color or black and white. Pricing and ordering information is posted on GAO's website, http://www.gao.gov/ordering.htm. Place orders by calling (202) 512-6000, toll free (866) 801-7077, or TDD (202) 512-2537. Orders may be paid for using American Express, Discover Card, MasterCard, Visa, check, or money order. Call for additional information.
Connect with GAO	Connect with GAO on Facebook, Flickr, Twitter, and YouTube. Subscribe to our RSS Feeds or E-mail Updates. Listen to our Podcasts. Visit GAO on the web at www.gao.gov.
To Report Fraud, Waste, and Abuse in Federal Programs	Contact: Website: http://www.gao.gov/fraudnet/fraudnet.htm E-mail: fraudnet@gao.gov Automated answering system: (800) 424-5454 or (202) 512-7470
Congressional Relations	Katherine Siggerud, Managing Director, siggerudk@gao.gov, (202) 512-4400, U.S. Government Accountability Office, 441 G Street NW, Room 7125, Washington, DC 20548
Public Affairs	Chuck Young, Managing Director, youngc1@gao.gov, (202) 512-4800 U.S. Government Accountability Office, 441 G Street NW, Room 7149 Washington, DC 20548